Divine

Nudges

of

Spirit

In spiritual support,

Nancy

Divine Nudges of Spirit

© 2010 by Nancy Fagen

Cover Image © Robert Garcia

Manufactured in the United States of America

This collection of writings is for the purpose of sharing with you some of the Divine Nudges of Spirit in my life with the intent that by expressing these experiences, I offer my readers, my family, and my friends a glimpse of who I am.

Especially for:

My daughter, Joy Hartley,
and her husband, Robert Garcia

My son, J Hartley, and his wife, Kerri Hartley

Loved ones Debbie Hartley
and her husband, Don Milner

The Ellis, Fagen, and Garcia families

And my beautiful grandchildren,
Camryn, Collin, Ellis, and Tatum.

Thank you for being my teachers of unconditional love.

Affectionately, Lulu

Table of Contents

Foreword

The first Sunday I found a truth teaching I could totally embrace, the spiritual director stated, "You may not believe everything you hear today, but you might hear something you already believe." There is a calling inside each of us to experience life from a higher perspective and to know we have come here on this plane of consciousness to be who we really are.

So many books challenge our thinking from a purely intellectual perspective. While I appreciate this approach on many levels, I most resonate to those books that give me a life experience of truth teaching. Nancy Fagen has done just that in writing this wonderful commentary on her life experiences. From the first page to the last, I was captivated by the realness of each vignette because I could relate on so many levels.

Change takes place in our lives only when we become aware that change needs to take place. Each moment of correct thinking moves us into a greater awareness of what needs to happen in our experience. Even the simplest decision can catapult us to a new dimension of awareness of the presence of a Higher Power in our lives.

Each page in *Divine Nudges of Spirit* offers a gentle wake-up call to a higher order of thought through the author's heightened awareness and personal transformation. You will see there is a law at work on the pages of this book, and while you may not believe everything you read, you may read something you already believe.

Share the joy of this collection with your friends and family. You may be pleasantly surprised at how well this book is received. I thoroughly enjoyed each and every moment. Thank you, Nancy, for sharing the Truth of you.

Maureen Hoyt

Introduction

For many years, I have felt the Divine Nudges of Spirit leading me to publish my writings. This book is my first response to those promptings.

The major portion of this material was written as a Science of Mind 400 class project in 1990 and has been lying dormant in an office closet until now. In an "aha" moment, I became aware that most of the material for my first book had already been written. I had only to take action in bringing it forth. I am reminded of the quote attributed to Jesus the Christ found in the Gospel of Thomas:

> If you bring forth what is within you, what you bring forth will save you. If you do not bring forth what is within you, what you do not bring forth will destroy you.

It took my awareness, decision, and willingness to allow Spirit to move through me to bring forth what is within me. It is my intent that you, the reader, gain inspiration for your life as you become increasingly aware of the Divine Nudges of Spirit expressing in, as, and through you.

In spiritual support,

Nancy Fagen

Chapter One

Divine Substance Everywhere

While walking on the beach, I observed a group of children playing near the shore. They were filling buckets with sand and building unique creations. I noticed one of the mothers was calling to them to move closer to where the family had situated.

The children emptied their buckets of sand and moved easily to the new spot. All the children, that is, except one.

He had not emptied his bucket and was attempting to drag it to the new location. Filled with wet sand, the bucket was very heavy, and he was quite small. It was indeed a struggle to move with such a heavy load.

I wondered why he was doing this when there was obviously no shortage of sand in the new location. In fact, he was literally walking on an abundance of sand as he dragged his heavy burden along.

I thought about how often I have felt the need to hang on to the buckets I once filled with sand, thinking they will be the only supply available to me even though I exist in a substance-filled universe.

Visible and invisible supply is everywhere present for me. As I become aware of this, I live in a more trusting and relaxing way, realizing substance is all around me. My role is to intelligently claim and readily accept what I desire to bring forth in my life. Divine substance is everywhere!

Imagining

"Imagination is more important than information."

– Albert Einstein

"What we now experience we may cease experiencing if we have the will and the imagination to set our vision in an opposite direction and hold it there. It is the office of the imagination to set the vision."

– Ernest Holmes

In everyday conversations, we often hear the following comments: Picture this, I can see it now, imagine that, what you see is what you get, and, it is all in how you look at it.

Imagination and visualization are very real parts of our lives. The Disney Corporation has named its creative employees "Imagineers." In a sense, we are all Imagineers, for we use our imagineering ability constantly.

What we see in our mind's eye becomes a reality by our use of this envisioning power. Many times, we casually use this power, unaware we are putting into motion the creation of what we imagine. We wonder why certain situations appear in our lives.

To create pleasant, harmonious, and prosperous living, we must see what we desire and place ourselves in the picture. By focusing on what we desire, feeling it is now real, we bring these effects into our experience.

We are our own Imagineers, and what we see is what we get. Imagine that!

Affirmation

I now use my imagination to envision joyful,
harmonious, and prosperous living.
I hold the focus firmly in place and know
all things necessary for its fulfillment are now
easily drawn to me.
In calm confidence, I move forward,
grateful this is so.

Rejoicing in All Good

". . . man cannot demonstrate his own good while wishing that someone else be kept from his good."

– Frederick Bailes

". . . I do not need to imitate anyone or to long for the good that belongs to another. All good is now mine and it now manifests in my experience."

– Ernest Holmes

One afternoon, I took a walk on a fishing pier near my home. I enjoyed watching the people and observing what they were catching. My interest heightened, however, when I became aware of the prosperity principles being expressed.

When someone caught a fish, not one of the other fishermen felt his good was taken from him. No one experienced a sense of personal injury when a new arrival appeared with fishing tackle and bait. No one packed his gear and left with resentment when someone else was successful in catching a fish.

On the contrary, when a fish was caught, the prevailing atmosphere was one of rejoicing. Everyone was filled with increased expectancy. They saw this as an indication that they, too, could succeed. They knew there was plenty for all.

As we rejoice with others when they receive their good, we open ourselves so that our good can easily flow to us. There is infinite abundance in the universe. Rejoice in all good!

Affirmation

I rejoice in all good.
As I do, I open the way for increased blessings
to appear in my life.
Gratefully, I now allow unlimited prosperity
to flow into all my experiences.

Using Our Connection

"There is a guidance for each of us, and by lowly listening we shall hear the right word."

– Ralph Waldo Emerson

"The Universal Mind contains all knowledge. To It, all things are possible. To us, as much is possible as we can conceive . . ."

– Ernest Holmes

An unlimited, constantly available source of information exists in Universal Mind, and each of us has ready access to it. The information we request can and does come from anywhere, anyone, anything, and at any time.

While watching a financial information television program, I thought of a question I wanted to ask. As I was writing the phone number for the call-in service, someone called in with the very same question. My answer was provided without my having to call.

As I was enjoying a facial in a spa, I heard someone in the next booth provide the very information I wanted to know. When I was in the process of making a decision on a legal matter, a friend loaned me a book that contained spiritual insights that were exactly right for me at the time.

When we expect information to be provided, we remain alert to recognizing it when it appears. Each of us is naturally and thoroughly equipped with a direct connection to Universal Mind. Just request, "Information, please!"

Affirmation

I am grateful everything I desire to know
is provided for me in easily recognizable ways
whenever I request it.

Acting on Decisions

"What you can do, or dream you can, begin it. Boldness has genius, power and magic in it. Only engage and then the mind grows heated. Begin, and then the work will be completed."

— Wolfgang von Goethe

"The correct understanding that Mind in Its unformed state can be called forth into individual use is the key to all proper mental and spiritual work from a practical viewpoint."

— Ernest Holmes

I was in a new contemporary office building for an appointment and decided to make a stop in the ladies' room. I could not find the light switch, and after searching inside, outside, and around the walls, I gave up looking. I decided I would maneuver my way by feeling the walls and doors.

To my amazement, when I stepped into the room, a bright array of lights turned on automatically. I had thought I needed a manual light switch when, in fact, none was necessary. All it took to turn on the lights was my decision to walk into the room and follow my decision with action.

As I thought about this event, I became more aware of the significance. What I may think is a necessary ingredient to attain a goal in my life may not be necessary at all. Deciding on the goal and moving forward in the face of any fear or doubt dispels the darkness and lights the way. Action is the turn-on!

Affirmation

I now allow my inner knowing to express as
right decisions and harmonious actions.
With calm assurance, I easily move forward,
accepting greater and greater good in my life.

Cooperating

". . . get into the habit of thinking about money as a never-ending event, which goes and comes, but is always there."

– Jerry Gillies

"Every day and every hour, we are meeting the eternal realities of life, and in such degree as we cooperate with these eternal realities in love, peace, in wisdom, and in joy–believing and receiving–we are automatically blessed."

– Ernest Holmes

As I reached for the quarter I had dropped, I recalled the suggestion: When you drop change, leave it there. This sends the message to your subconscious mind that there is plenty more coming in.

Further, it places the money into universal circulation and gives someone the opportunity to rejoice over finding it. I did just that and went on my way.

That evening, when I walked into the ladies' room of a restaurant, I was amazed to find a one-dollar bill lying in the middle of the floor. I used it as part of my tip. A few days later when my son and I were in the same restaurant, the thought occurred to me to replace the dollar I had found earlier. I did so, putting it in the same spot and wondering what would happen.

That night, during a phone conversation with my daughter, she mentioned she had just found a twenty-dollar bill in the restaurant where she was working. The spiritual laws of circulation and increase are indeed alive and well! 'Round and 'round it all goes!

Affirmation

*I now peacefully move into an ever-increasing awareness
and understanding of the eternal realities of life.
I willingly and joyfully cooperate with Universal Law
and am automatically blessed.*

Chapter Two

Casual Is Causal

Driving home from a conference, I casually mentioned to a friend, "I'm ready for an angel to come for my white wicker furniture." I was making a geographic move in a week and had already sold many items. The only major item left to sell was my white wicker furniture.

When I returned to my home, there was a message on the answering machine from a woman saying she was interested in buying a small television for her son. She wanted to come look at the one I had advertised.

We arranged a time, and while she was looking at the television, she spotted the white wicker furniture. She immediately expressed an interest in buying it.

We arrived at a price, and she said her husband would return at five o'clock with a truck. I agreed, and she left.

A few minutes after five o'clock, the doorbell rang. When I opened the door, a man introduced himself to me. "My name is Angel," he said. "I've come for the furniture." Feeling amazed but appearing calm, I said, "Yes, of course, please come in."

In a flash of awareness, I recalled my comment to my friend the day before. After loading the furniture on his truck, Angel presented me with a check, saying, "And this check is good."

I answered, "I'm sure it is!" The check had his name, Angel, on it and was beautifully decorated with small cherubs.

When I think of this event, I am reminded that any thought I think–expressed or unexpressed, however casual–is indeed *causal* to my experience.

Changing Direction

"We enjoy and even thrill to the godlike possibilities we see in ourselves in peak moments. And yet we simultaneously shiver with weakness, awe, and fear before these same possibilities. Fear of knowing is very deeply a fear of doing."

— Abraham Maslow

"All doubt and fear must go and in their place must come faith and confidence, for we shall be led by the Spirit into all good."

— Ernest Holmes

While on vacation at a winter resort, I decided to take a ski lesson as a reminder of proper techniques before enjoying the trails on the mountains. For ease and coordination in changing direction while skiing, the instructor suggested I simply look in the direction I want to go. He instructed me not to look at my skis or think about what I was doing.

To my amazement, everything fell perfectly into place. My body and skis changed automatically, corresponding to the direction I had turned my head to look at the destination.

On a nearby slope, vision-impaired skiers were learning the same process. Their instructor skied backwards and talked them toward the direction they were to go. In complete trust and faith, they moved in the direction of his voice.

I became aware of how this same process works in all parts of our experience. To change the direction of our lives, we simply listen to our inner knowing and follow in complete trust. As a result, everything falls perfectly into place.

Affirmation

I now listen to my inner knowing and
follow it in complete trust.
By acting in faith and confidence,
I watch everything in my life fall perfectly in place.

Honoring Desires

"Desire in all instances is a hint of the thing we ought to have."

– Emma Curtis Hopkins

"Know that the greater abundance of every good thing you are bringing out in your life, the more perfectly you are satisfying the Divine Urge within you."

– Ernest Holmes

As a child, I recall hearing that to have what I desired was not always possible and somehow not right. It seemed this was how things were supposed to be, and the more readily I accepted this fact, the easier my life would be.

Over time, I have come to understand that desires are the inner Spirit yearning for fuller expression. Discontent, which sometimes prompts desire, is telling us life can be better. Our desires are telling us how to connect with our greater good.

If our desires do no harm to ourselves or others, we have a spiritual obligation to honor them. They are Divine Nudges of Spirit seeking fuller expression through us. By virtue of having a desire, we awaken to the reality that fulfillment is possible. It is ready for our acceptance.

By connecting with the desires of the Divine Self within us, we nurture and fulfill our purpose to live life more prosperously. Honor your desires!

Affirmation

I now lovingly honor my desires.
As I do, I am more perfectly satisfying
the Divine Urge within me for
greater expressions of good in my life.

Living in the Now

". . . today well-lived, makes every yesterday a dream of happiness, and every tomorrow a vision of hope. Look well, therefore, to this day!"

– Sanskrit Poem

"We should also erase the thoughts of yesterday that would rob us of today's happiness."

– Ernest Holmes

I sometimes watch *I Love Lucy* reruns on television and thoroughly enjoy laughing with Lucy. In one of the episodes, Lucy, Ricky, and friends boarded a cruise ship for a vacation.

While waving goodbye to little Ricky, Lucy decided she wanted to hug her son once more before leaving, and she disembarked. Unfortunately, in the midst of the embrace, her skirt caught on the chain of a nearby bicycle. She tried everything imaginable to loosen it but with no success. Too late, she removed her skirt and ran for the ship. It had sailed without her.

We, too, sometimes complicate our lives unnecessarily, caught on bicycle chains of the past. We attempt to go back to the glorified good old days and miss the opportunities to create better new days in the present.

How much easier our lives are when we look only forward and accept the now. All aboard!

Affirmation

I peacefully see every facet of my life
as a continuously flowing stream of good.
I now choose to live well in this day,
fully experiencing the joys of each moment.

In with the New

"Nothing can ever be lost through spiritual release. Instead, your own good and the good of all concerned is much freer to move into your life. Through release, your power of attracting good is greatly increased."

— Catherine Ponder

"If the organs of the body followed the average tactics of [people] in acquisitive habits, if the lungs hoarded the air they take in, if the heart kept the fresh blood stored within its walls, refusing to allow it to circulate, if the stomach retained the food taken in for nourishment, what a static condition we would have!"

— Ernest Holmes

I recall a specific time in my life when I decided I was ready for desired changes. Knowing that through release my power for attracting good is greatly increased, I began observing areas of my life where I could release that which was not nurturing me.

The benefit of doing this was clearly brought to my attention when I hesitatingly gave away a blue chenille robe that had been a favorite for many years. The threadbare condition was living proof it had served its purpose. I had kept it because it was so comfortably familiar–like a second skin.

Surprisingly, and to my delight, the very next day after I gave it away, a package arrived in the mail. It was an early birthday gift–a gift of beautiful blue pajamas and a matching robe!

As I placed the new items in my closet, I again reflected on the law of circulation and how I had created the vacuum for the new garments now in my closet. If ever I doubt the law of circulation, I recall this event and know that releasing the old is indeed the first step toward receiving the new.

Affirmation

Intelligently and calmly, I decide to keep that which nurtures and supports me in moving forward in my greater good. I lovingly bless and gratefully release that which has served its purpose in my life, whatever it may have been. As I do this, my consciousness is filled and overflowing with the newness of increased clarity, prosperity, and peace.

Selecting and Acting

"You are in a spiritual universe to act, decide, and select, and upon your decision rests your experience."

– Raymond Charles Barker

". . . we should daily practice correct thinking. We should decide what we wish to have happen in our lives."

– Ernest Holmes

From my balcony, I glanced at the swimming pool crowded with summer swimmers. Wondering whether swimming laps would be possible for me, I decided to go to the pool and make the attempt.

As I began swimming, I noticed that when the people in the pool realized my intent, they gladly cooperated by giving me space. One young man voluntarily accepted the responsibility of keeping the small children on the other side of the pool. Some of the swimmers left for sunning or lunch.

What earlier appeared to be a crowded pool was suddenly open. The way was clear for me to accomplish what I had decided to do.

By just doing it, I made a clear statement of my desire and intent, inviting the cooperation of the universe to support me in my decision. Just do it!

Affirmation

I clearly define my goals.
Every decision is easily and peacefully made
as I move harmoniously forward into right action
and perfect order.

Chapter
Three

The Power of Declaration

It was the day before my daughter was to arrive for her wedding. I had bought some flowers, food, and supplies for the condo where she would be staying.

As I entered the condo, I realized the carpet desperately needed to be cleaned. It had been acceptable when I chose this unit and reserved it, but the time between then and now had left its mark.

I stood in the middle of the living area and with great feeling and determination declared, "This carpet has to be cleaned!"

I quickly put away the items I had brought with me and began my walk to the manager's office. I was halfway there when I heard a truck pull up to the building I had

just left. I could not believe my eyes! It was a carpet-cleaning truck, and the workers were taking equipment to the condo next door to the one I had reserved for my daughter.

I walked quickly to the office and explained to the manager that the carpet had to be cleaned immediately. The manager stated there was absolutely no way she could have the carpet cleaned without the owner's permission, and there was not enough time to get in touch with the owner.

Fortunately, the woman in charge of the cleaning was also there. I suggested they both go with me to look at the unit. When they saw it, they agreed this had to be done right away and agreed to work out the details later. They talked to the owner of the carpet-cleaning business and arranged to have it cleaned immediately after he finished with the one next door.

As I thought about this event, I realized I had made my declaration with great feeling, which had produced immediate desired results. "This carpet has to be cleaned!" was my effective affirmative prayer, and the universe responded immediately. Gratefully, I left the situation with a confirmation that the universe delivers what is impressed upon it when I make my declarations.

Accepting

"Make your environment work for you. Go first class in everything you do. You can't afford to go any other way."

– David J. Schwartz

"We must be specific in what we do, while at the same time never outlining how it shall be done. Remember we are dealing with Intelligence."

– Ernest Holmes

Somewhere in the process of my coat being placed on a hanger, the hot towels offered before lunch, the choice of several entrees, the cloth napkin spread over my tray, and more than ample leg and elbow room, I realized something: I was in the middle of a demonstration.

At the suggestion of a prosperity consciousness teacher, I had listed a number of items I desired to demonstrate. One of the items was to fly first class. I recall thinking I would need extra money to accomplish this.

Creative Intelligence worked it out in a different way. My daughter accepted employment with a major airline, and I was given special flying privileges. When I began using these benefits, I discovered that not only did they offer minimal fare, they also offered first-class accommodations when available.

I took the suggestion of the prosperity teacher on his word, and Creative Intelligence took me on my word. Divine Law is our all-knowing servant. Why not go first class?

Affirmation

I deserve the very best in life
and now lovingly allow myself to accept it.
By cooperating with spiritual laws,
I enjoy ease and lightness in all my living.

Choosing Happiness

"Unhappiness is based on a logical system of beliefs."

– Barry Neil Kaufman

"We are some part of this creative order and we cannot change our nature. We had better use it constructively than destructively; in happiness rather than misery."

– Ernest Holmes

Trigger-happy describes the quality of a person who freely and frequently pulls a trigger, usually that of a gun. We, too, are sometimes trigger-happy when we freely and frequently pull a trigger that evokes certain emotional states from the past. We do this by allowing the feelings associated with past experiences to enter into the present moment.

These feelings often come forth when hearing a song, looking at a photograph, recalling a past event or location, and numerous similar instances. Many times, we are unaware of the patterns of association we have established.

When we do become aware, we can change the reaction these triggers evoke, replacing an unpleasant response with a pleasant one. The event is then viewed from a new perspective. A rainy day no longer dampens our spirits. We evoke the feeling of being nourished by appreciating the rain's natural purification process of the air and its feeding of the luscious green growth of the earth.

By consciously choosing to evoke desired emotions, we become trigger-happy in the truest sense.

Affirmation

I now choose to accept increased happiness in my life.
As I lighten up, I move into a
greater sense of enlightenment,
experiencing an ever increasing enjoyment of living.

Feeling Unlimited

"As you enter into the mood of opulence, all things necessary for the abundant life will come to pass."

— Joseph Murphy

"No person whose entire time is spent in the contemplation of limitation can demonstrate freedom from such limitation."

— Ernest Holmes

When shopping for clothes, there was a time I automatically went to the reduced items advertised as bargains. Once, I purchased an outfit simply because it was fifty percent off the original price. It did not fit well, and I never really felt good in it. Still, I wore it a few times before I knew I deserved better.

During another shopping trip some time later, I admired a beautiful silk jacket on display. When I tried it on, it fit perfectly, and I felt good in it. I also selected matching accessories I liked.

The collection was quite pricey, but I decided to purchase the items anyway. As I reached for my wallet, the salesclerk informed me my selections were available at a reduced cost because of an upcoming sales promotion.

In this experience, I did not limit my choices. I selected what I liked and wanted and was willing to pay the price. I consider this a good deal not purchased with bargain-basement thinking.

Affirmation

I now move into a greater sense of feeling unlimited.
In this consciousness, I automatically draw
all things necessary for a more
prosperous life into my experience.

Letting Go

"Whatever is true . . . honorable . . . just . . . pure . . . lovely . . . gracious . . . think about these things . . ."

– Philippians 4:8

"Should we learn to contemplate those things which are desirable and to forget the rest, we would soon overcome fear through faith."

– Ernest Holmes

When I telephoned the World Ministry of Prayer, I was greeted by a calm recording telling me to wait for the next available practitioner. The voice suggested while waiting I begin to release my challenge.

At the time, I was most distressed by this suggestion. If I waited much longer and began releasing the challenge, I would forget all the important details I wanted to tell someone.

However, as the soft music played and I calmed myself, I realized how desperately I wanted to hold on. This challenge was mine. I had created and nurtured it with a lot of energy.

During the conversation and spiritual mind treatment (affirmative prayer), I became willing to release and clear. Later that evening, I laughed at myself as I saw the humor and truth of the situation.

The more I laughed, the more I was ready to release. The truth became clear as I was willing to let go of the challenge—especially the details.

Affirmation

I now willingly choose to accept peace,
clear thinking, and happiness as the
only theme in my life.
All my experiences reflect love, peace, and joy
as I live in complete harmony with my Divine nature.

Relaxing into New Dimensions

"Celebrate the joy of the moment."

— Irene Allemano

". . . the human is really Divine but will ever evolve into newer and better states of conscious being."

— Ernest Holmes

In the Broadway musical *Annie*, Annie is invited to stay as a special guest in the Warbucks mansion. With the visit arranged, she leaves her accustomed environment of the orphanage.

Upon arrival at the mansion, Annie is asked what she would like to do. After carefully examining the new environment, she decisively replies that she will start with the windows and then do the floors.

Sometimes, when we move ourselves into new dimensions of living, we are uncomfortable without the familiarities of the past, however unpleasant they may have been. We often miss fully experiencing the joy of the moment—the beginning of a new and greater dimension.

However, as we unfold in spiritual awareness, we continually find ourselves moving upward in the spiral of life. It is the natural result of our spiritual unfolding.

Affirmation

*I now easily and naturally relax
into new and richer dimensions of living,
celebrating the joy of each moment.*

Chapter
Four

Catch of the Day

As I walked along the shore, I watched the crews of several fishing boats lower their nets into the sea. With anticipation and expectancy, they began fishing for their catch of the day.

When fishermen pull in the nets at the end of their day, they evaluate the catch, keep what is of value, and discard the leftovers. The seagulls know this and follow closely.

We, too, cast our nets upon the living waters to bring in our catch of the day. The sea of unformed substance surrounds us at all times. Our net is our consciousness—our thought and feeling atmosphere.

What we draw to ourselves is the effect of this atmosphere. We can look at our catch and decide what we want to sustain and what we want to change. We do this by changing our prevailing thoughts and feelings.

The more we objectively evaluate the effects, the more peacefully and intelligently we set new causes. We can then cast new nets of consciousness upon the living waters and draw to us a new catch of the day.

Befriending the World

"Yes, I joyfully affirm that I am on friendly terms with a friendly world. The universe is my friend, and all people and all of nature's forces and manifestations are supportive of me."

— Roy Eugene Davis

"Think of the whole world as your friend, but you must also be the friend of the whole world."

— Ernest Holmes

The rental car I was driving began to sputter and cough. Coasting to the side of the road, I realized I had miscalculated the distance the supply of gas would take me. There I was without fuel on an interstate highway and no exit in sight.

At first, I was not certain what to do. Then, I remembered and affirmed that everything I request is always provided for me in perfect ways. At the moment, my request was a ride to a service station.

I knew action on my part was in order, and I signaled the driver of the first approaching semi truck. He gave me a ride to the nearest gasoline supply. When I offered to pay him, he told me to pass on the help when I could. He was happy to be of help.

At the service station, an employee gladly gave me a return ride to the car, supplied it with gasoline, and followed me back to the service station making sure I arrived safely. We live in a supportive, friendly universe with active angels on patrol!

Affirmation

Everything in my experience reflects harmony, love, and peace. I am grateful for a friendly universe that supports good for all.

Clearing

"Cluttered closets mean a cluttered mind. As you clean the closet, say to yourself, 'I am cleaning out the closets of my mind.'"

– Louise Hay

"It is necessary that we release all thought—as well as things—that clutter up our lives."

– Ernest Holmes

Knowing what to keep and what to give away is one of the most important ongoing processes in life. Everything in our environment is a result of our choices. If we want to take inventory of how clear or cluttered our minds and lives are, a good place to look is in our closets—however painful the thought and act of doing so!

For several years, I kept two coats that were no longer useful to me. They had served their purpose in the cooler climate where I once lived. When I removed them from the closet, I realized I no longer liked the colors. Besides, moths and mildew had found a home in both coats over the years.

Keeping what no longer serves us is a clear message that we are not ready for new and increased good in our lives. The universe responds accordingly.

Let's examine our closet consciousness, clear the clutter, and make room for today's good!

Affirmation

*I now clear the clutter from my mind
and my environment. As I do, I readily invite and
welcome new and greater good into my life.*

Expressing

". . . the urge to do and be that which is the noblest, the most beautiful of which we are capable, is the creative impulse of every high achievement . . ."

– Paramahansa Yogananda

"There is an urge to express in all people, and this urge, operating through the channels of Creative Mind, looses energy into action. Back of all this is the impulse of Spirit to express."

– Ernest Holmes

Our creative impulse, inherently present within, must be expressed. It is an integral part of the creative force that flows through the universe. We are either expressing in productive, appropriate ways or in ways that are non-productive and inappropriate for our highest good. The only choice we have is how to direct this creative flow in our lives—to express or depress.

Not honoring the creative impulse is unhealthy and dangerous. If we attempt to hold down the creative part of us, it shows up in depressing ways. It may express in dis-ease of the body, the mis-use of substances, or nervous, scattered energy.

As we honor our creative impulses and stay in harmony with our inner knowing of how to express the impulses of Spirit, we are in tune with that which is continually flowing and being. Express the best!

Affirmation

I now lovingly honor my creative impulses.
I am always in harmony with perfect expressions
for my highest good as I stay in tune with Spirit,
continually flowing through me.
I express the best in all areas of my life.

Living in Mind

". . . one continually attracts to himself forces and influences most akin to those of his own life . . . determined by the thoughts and emotions he habitually entertains . . ."

— Ralph Waldo Trine

"We live in Mind and It can return to us only what we think into It."

— Ernest Holmes

Imagine a loudspeaker attached to the top of your head. Through this speaker, every thought and feeling is broadcast to everyone in the world. Nothing is censored unless you negate your message by replacing it with new thoughts and feelings.

This is what is happening 24 hours a day from us to Universal Mind at every moment of our lives. Nothing is left out.

I recall being in a store looking for towels that would coordinate with my bathroom. As I selected the items I wanted, I noticed towels of a lesser quality were reduced in price. For a moment, I considered exchanging the first selection for the reduced items.

I knew they were not what I wanted, and the difference in cost was minimal. Somewhere at that time in my thought pattern was an old message telling me I had better settle for less than I desired, my enjoyment was not important, and I may need the difference in money for something else. I stayed with my first decision and immediately affirmed that I refuse to settle for less than I desire, my enjoyment is important, and all my needs are abundantly met.

Thoughts and feelings are the message—you are on the air!

Affirmation

I identify with the Power behind all things.
By keeping my thoughts and feelings aligned with my Divine nature, I naturally attract peaceful, prosperous, and purposeful living in all areas of my life.

Unifying

A friend and I had discussed the importance of remaining alert to the whisperings of Spirit. As we parted, she advised me to keep my antenna up.

On walking to my car, I was very much aware that its radio antenna had not been working for several weeks. It was designed to work automatically; however, turning on the radio brought no results.

Several days later, while driving in the city and waiting for a signal light to turn green, I noticed the car in the next lane was the same model and make as mine. Its antenna was up. I looked at the other antenna, then spoke to the one on my car. "Okay, antenna. That's what you're supposed to be doing!"

Instantaneously, the antenna on my car smoothly moved up to full height. It was completely obedient to my command, and I able to receive clear music.

Every time I see an antenna, I am reminded of the interconnectedness of all things and the power of my word. Keep your antenna up!

Affirmation

My word has power. I now use this power
to bring forth greater good in my world.
I see and appreciate the interconnectedness of all things
and my oneness with the Universe.
I am in harmony with all life.

Chapter
Five

Setting Ourselves Free

Would you like your life to be different? Let me share with you some thoughts from the prologue of *Illusions* by Richard Bach. I have created the ritual of reading from this prologue on New Year's Day, although it is certainly appropriate for our spiritual journey at any time.

The story is told of a village of creatures living along the bottom of a great crystal river. Even though the current swept silently over them, all the creatures clung tightly to the twigs and rocks at the bottom of the river, for clinging was their way of life.

Resisting the current was what each had learned from birth. One creature, bored and tired of clinging, let go and refused to cling again.

In time, the current lifted him up, free from the bottom. The others who were still clinging called him a Messiah, come to save us all. To this he replied, "I am no more Messiah than you. The river delights to set us free, if only we dare let go. Our true work is this adventure."

In *This Thing Called Life*, Ernest Holmes wrote:

> Today, realizing there is nothing in my past that can rise above me, nothing in my future that can menace the unfoldment of my experience, life shall be an eternal adventure, an unfolding experience of greater and better experiences. Evolution is onward, upward, forward, outward, expansive.

Now, I ask myself, where in my life am I clinging to that which does not nurture me? Where do I need to let go and move forward, trusting the Law manifests for me according to my belief?

You may want to ask yourself these questions, then listen to your intuition as it responds. I affirm for each of you a nurturing, expanding, and joyous adventure of embracing your own infinite potential!

Believing

"...first form the ideal conception of our object...then affirm that our knowledge of the Law is sufficient reason for a calm expectation of a corresponding result, and that therefore all necessary conditions will come to us in due order."

— *Thomas Troward*

"We must have a receptive and positive faith in the evidence of things not seen with the physical eye but which are eternal in the heavens."

— *Ernest Holmes*

When working as a salesperson, I decided to visualize my name at the top of the monthly sales chart for the purpose of increasing my income. I found a photograph from a previous month when my name had been at the top of the chart and began imprinting it on my mind.

The process started working. Sales came quickly and easily. However, cancellations also started coming with great regularity. Since cancellations were not shown on the chart, I demonstrated exactly what I had envisioned—my name at the top.

I realized I needed to look beyond this spiritual short-sightedness I had set in motion and began visualizing my income increasing. I had placed myself in the role of directing the demonstration, when in truth, my role is to select wisely what I desire and to release the desire to Creative Intelligence to work out. That is Its very purpose; mine is to know and believe.

When I believe in the final outcome, the way to get there is always automatically provided.

Affirmation

I now choose wisely that which I desire for my greater good. I plant this intention and release it to Creative Intelligence for manifestation in my life. I am at peace.

Focusing

"There is only one wisdom; it is to understand the thought by which all things are steered through all things."

– Heraclitus, 500 B.C.

"Concentration of thought is not an effort to compel, but the desire to permit the stream of Creative Energy to take definite form. We concentrate our attention. The Law creates the form."

– Ernest Holmes

During my childhood, I often ventured with my father on his sport-fishing boat. Once, on returning from an ocean outing, he asked me to steer the boat while he adjusted the engine.

My instructions were to keep my eyes on the lighthouse and steer toward it. He knew this was all that was necessary for me to steer us safely through the channel to our destination.

I eagerly accepted this task. I agreed I would keep my eyes on the lighthouse.

I concentrated well for a while, but then I allowed myself to become distracted by surrounding scenery on the coast. I was again instructed to keep my eyes on the lighthouse. I had wandered off course.

At the time, I was not aware of the universal truth being expressed. As long as I kept my focus on the destination, I automatically steered toward it. When I became distracted, I moved off course.

As I keep my mind's eye focused on that which I desire, I invite all things necessary to support the manifestation. As I keep my eyes on the Truth, Spirit makes sure I stay on course.

Affirmation

*I now keep my mind's eye focused on what I desire
to manifest in my life. I stay on course for
my highest good and best expression and
permit increased good to flow into all my experiences.*

Loving the Self

". . . the position of the Universal Mind towards us is always the reflection of our own attitude...we can then cheerfully look upon it as our ever-present Friend, providing all good counsel . . ."

– Thomas Troward

"We should approach the Law normally and naturally and with a sense of ease . . . consider the Law and the Spirit as friends . . . This is the natural unfoldment of Reality through [us]."

– Ernest Holmes

In Greek mythology, Narcissus fell totally in love with his own image reflected in a pool of water. After wasting away from unsatisfied desire, he was transformed into the flower that bears his name.

Unlike Narcissus, our desires can be fulfilled. By being in love with our highest Self—the God Presence within—our desires assist us in unfolding the petals of our own inner beauty and purpose.

In personal growth seminars, mirrors are often used to intensify the effectiveness of affirmations. There seems to be a magical power in the process.

Intrigued with this process, I began thinking of my mirror image as my God image—my subconscious, all-knowing servant—reflecting what I choose to be. I think of this image as my best friend who totally supports me. Its very nature is to do so.

If, at any time, I doubt this creative power is there for me, I look in a mirror. I remind myself that my obedient servant and best friend is within and always ready to carry out my choices.

The more I love God in me, the more perfection I see in my world. My world is a true mirror of who I am.

Affirmation

I love God within me naturally and with a sense of ease.
I tenderly nurture the unfolding of my own inner beauty
and see greater good reflected in my world.

Speaking Up

". . . ask, and it shall be given you . . ."

– Luke 11:9

"We should recognize the Power we are working with— realizing our Oneness with It—and then we should ask for what we wish and take it."

– Ernest Holmes

While staying in a hotel and relying on other people for transportation, I was reminded of the importance of making my requests known. I was aware the hotel van was available for rides to and from the airport and assumed it only provided that service.

Later the thought came to me to inquire about the van taking me other places. The driver stated this was possible and that I should make my request known to personnel at the hotel desk.

One phone call was all it took to have the van accessible to take me wherever I wanted to go. Not only was the van available, the drivers were willing and happy to cooperate with my requests and went out of their way to help.

I was reminded Universal Law is here for me. My part is to make my requests known. Every need was supplied easily and happily, and the people involved appreciated the bonus I gladly gave them.

Make your requests known to the Law. Speak up!

Affirmation

I now unhesitatingly speak my requests
to Infinite Intelligence.
In calm assurance, I know all things necessary
for perfect fulfillment are drawn to me
easily and harmoniously.
For this, I am grateful.

Using the Power

". . . all spirit is concentrated at any point in space that we may choose to fix our thought upon."

— Thomas Troward

"The energy of Mind, like other natural energies, already exists. We merely use It . . ."

— Ernest Holmes

I stood near the ocean with a group of other viewers watching the local effects of a powerful, off-shore hurricane. As I observed the awesome surges of current and waves forcefully pounding the sea wall and pier, I felt overwhelmed by the display. I realized this was but a symbol of the tremendous, creative power of the universe that is already established.

I became more aware of a connection with this universal power, knowing each of us is a focal point for its full use at all times. Consciously or unconsciously, each of us is using it in our lives.

Our role is to choose–wisely and intelligently–how we direct this creative force. As we grow in spiritual understanding, we become more knowledgeable of perfect ways to use this power for the good of all. It is already there for us!

Affirmation

I am a point of expression through which
the creative energy of the universe flows.
By my right thinking, I now consciously and
wisely direct this creative power to produce
increased good for myself and all others.

Chapter
Six

Sea Shells

While walking along the shore, I often reflect on the abundance and variety of shells placed there by the action of the surf and tides. I imagine the sea creatures who once needed these shells spend no time bemoaning the fact that releasing is a necessary part of their expansion of life.

Naturally and willingly, they release what is no longer appropriate for their growth. They experience neither concern nor interest as to whether their discarded shells are claimed by collectors or disintegrated into the natural cycle of the sea and shore.

Like sea creatures, we outgrow the shells of our former stages of life. What was once necessary and appropriate for our support needs to be viewed from a fresh perspective.

The good of the past is not sufficient for today. As we move from good to greater good, we must naturally and willingly discard that which no longer serves us in our ongoing growth. As we do so, we make room for our greater good to appear.

Knowing

"If certain things do not come at certain expected times in the way you wish, do not consider it a failure . . . stand firm in the faith that something much better is on the way and will appear at the right time."

– Catherine Ponder

"Break down everything except the One Perfect Power, which is not contingent upon any place, person, condition, time of year, or anything but Itself."

– Ernest Holmes

When I decided to travel for several months, I placed my condominium in a rental program for the time I would be away. I affirmed the appropriate renters would enjoy being in it and that I would benefit from the rental proceeds during my travels.

I was told by the rental manager that there were no promises for rentals since this time of the year was considered off-season. I refused to accept that, knowing there is no off-season in Divine Mind.

Just before leaving for my travels, I was notified that a short-term rental had been canceled with no immediate replacement. I again affirmed that appropriate renters would enjoy being in my condominium. I left for my trip.

When my mail reached me a week later, there was a check for a month's rent. The short-term cancellation had cleared the way for a much better rental. What appeared at first to be an obstacle was simply a signal of greater good on the way.

Affirmation

In calm trust, I know I am now encompassed
by perfect life, by all power, and by all guidance.
I gratefully accept my supply of all good.

Living in Wholeness

"Choosing love, joy, and freedom. I am healthy, whole, and complete."

— Louise Hay

"The life forces flow freely, peacefully, and harmoniously through every atom of my body. I am complete and perfect now."

— Ernest Holmes

One of our inalienable constitutional rights is the right to the pursuit of happiness. Some people never get beyond the pursuit. A higher right, however, is our Divine right to accept happiness now, giving up the wasted energy spent in the unnecessary painful process of pursuit.

In a similar way, some of us never get beyond seeking the Presence of God. We are so caught up in the search that we miss the joy of being in the Presence.

If we are to go beyond the seeking, we must recognize the Presence of God already in, as, and through us. As we relax into the Presence, we can safely let go of the need to constantly search for completion.

We are now perfect, whole, and complete spiritual beings having a human experience. Our acceptance of happiness and perfection is all that is necessary for us to live in this consciousness. From this state of being, we naturally and peacefully live beyond pursuing and seeking.

Affirmation

I totally accept and believe I am whole, perfect, and complete right now. As I relax into the Divine Presence of perfection within, I naturally and peacefully live in a consciousness of wholeness.

Receiving

"If someone says to you, 'I want to give you something' and it is at all usable, take it. If it isn't usable, take it anyway and give it to someone else, because that's the way card party prizes circulate."

— Raymond Charles Barker

"Lowell said, 'The gift without the giver is bare,' and it is just as true that there can be no gift without a receiver."

— Ernest Holmes

Very often, I have blocked my good without even being aware I was doing it. Many times in the past, I refused compliments, gifts, and favors from well-meaning friends and relatives.

I was not only unwilling to receive, I was also blocking good from others by not allowing them the opportunity to give and feel good about it.

When I became aware of how many times I said, "No thanks!" to others, I consciously decided to change my attitude. The next items offered to me were a pink scarf and a small green vase. I felt an exciting awareness when I consciously accepted these gifts with gratitude and said, "Thank you."

The giver was able to know the joy of giving. I was willing to open to the joy of receiving.

I would not have chosen those items for myself. However, I kept them for a while as a reminder to stay in the consciousness of being ready and willing to receive good from wherever it comes. Simply say, "Thank you!"

Affirmation

I am in complete harmony with the giving and receiving nature of the universe.
Joyfully, I accept my good from wherever it appears.

Tuning In

"When one comes into and lives continually in the full, conscious realization of oneness with the Infinite Life and Power, then all else follows."

— Ralph Waldo Trine

". . . our belief sets the limit to our demonstration of a Principle which, of Itself, is without limit . . . it is not a question of Its willingness, nor of Its ability. It is entirely a question of our own receptivity."

— Ernest Holmes

I was once the teacher in a seventh-grade class. One Friday, the students' reward for the week was to enjoy a video of *The Wizard of Oz*.

The first few minutes of the showing went as planned with all of us enjoying it. Too soon, however, came an interruption in reception.

At this point, I was not sure what to do. In the midst of the children's expressed disappointment, I decided a spiritual mind treatment (affirmative prayer) was in order.

I wanted to remedy this situation quickly. As I prayed, I thought of trying a different channel on the television. Knowing this would be unusual, I followed my intuition. To everyone's delight, the reception was perfectly restored, and we continued enjoying the video.

I was reminded that this is how demonstrations happen. We do our spiritual mind treatments, then move on the thought of action coming to us.

We are an integral part of the demonstration. As we keep our reception clear, we know what to do to keep the picture clear.

Affirmation

I am receptive to and in tune with my inner knowing.
I continuously express clear thinking and right action
as I allow unlimited good to flow through me
into my world of events.

Waking to the Real Self

"What we are looking for is what is looking."

– Saint Francis of Assisi

"We are on the path of experience, just waking to the real fact of our true being."

– Ernest Holmes

One afternoon, I drove to at least six auto shops looking for a tire to fit my car. Meeting with no success, I returned home, feeling somewhat weary and defeated.

Later that evening, I thought about a tire someone had given me a few months ago. I attempted at one time to use it, but the rim attached to the tire did not fit the car. I decided to place it in the trunk until I found someone who could use it.

Up to this point, my thinking was limited to only one possibility—that of using both the tire and the attached rim. I suddenly became aware of the possibility that the tire alone may fit the rim already on the car. It did. What I had been driving around all afternoon looking for was riding around with me in the trunk of my car!

As we rid ourselves of limited thinking and see ourselves as complete beings now, we open to the perfection within.

Affirmation

I now open my awareness to the true nature
of Divine perfection within. I recognize and embrace
my oneness with all good, knowing I am perfect, whole,
and complete this day and every day.

About the
Author

Reverend Nancy Fagen, Ph.D., ordained pastor of the Jacksonville, Florida, Center for Spiritual Living, inspires readers with practical ways to live from their highest potential. She holds a Ph.D. from the Institute of Transpersonal Psychology and is a faculty mentor in the ITP Global Program, teaching students throughout the world in a distance learning graduate degree program.

Successfully blending Science of Mind principles with transpersonal psychology theories, Rev. Dr. Fagen presents workshops, classes, lectures, and writings that reflect her extensive experience in both arenas. You are invited to join with many others who benefit from her clear and uplifting writings.

For more information visit www.nancyfagen.com or write to Post Office Box 565, St.Augustine, FL 32085-0565. Email: DivineNudgesOfSpirit@nancyfagen.com.